SPEAKING OF GOD

AN INTRODUCTORY CONVERSATION ABOUT HOW CHRISTIANS TALK ABOUT GOD

ROBERT D. CORNWALL

Topical Line Drives
#50

Energion Publications
Gonzalez, Florida
2023

ISBN: 978-1-63199-854-6
eISBN: 978-1-63199-855-3

Energion Publications
P. O. Box 841
Gonzalez, FL 32560

pubs@energion.com
energion.com

INTRODUCTION

Humans have been pondering, perhaps since the beginning of human consciousness, whether something lies beyond the world of our senses. How and when religion emerged remains an open question, but perhaps John Calvin is correct when he suggested that we possess within us a sense of the divine (*sensus divinitas*). I have long found that rationale for the origin of religion compelling. It's not proof, but it does have some explanatory power. That is because even though humans may frame their understanding of the divine differently, every culture seems to have developed some form of religion. For some God is an all-powerful being who controls all things while for others God is the fellow traveler who walks with us through life, guiding and consoling us but not controlling things. God has been described as the "unmoved mover" or first cause (Aristotle) and the "ground of being (Paul Tillich). God is understood by some as being immanent, close at hand, while for others God is transcendent (wholly other). God might be understood to be deeply engaged with us, even as our partner in life (relational theology), or completely uninvolved with the universe other than getting things started (deism). In popular culture, we often hear God referred to as the "Man Upstairs," an image that conjures in our minds the picture of an old man with a long white beard. On the other hand, one can refer to God as the "womb of being." These are but descriptions of God embraced by Christians. There is, to be honest, an understandable tendency to envision God in our own image, having human traits and characteristics, only better. This is not a problem as long as we understand that these descriptions are metaphors and should not be taken literally.

While Christians look to Scripture for guidance when it comes to our beliefs about God, we don't read Scripture in a vacuum. We often make use of philosophical concepts and culturally laden vocabulary to interpret and express what we find in Scripture and what we consider to be foundational. Many of our foundational Christian beliefs have been influenced by Greek philosophy, especially Plato and Aristotle. This is true, whether we acknowledge this inheritance or not. The reason for this is that since the earliest times, as the Christian movement moved out from Jerusalem and its Jewish origins, Christians have sought out language and concepts that could be used to further our theological discussion and definitions. That continues to this day. Even theologians who have chosen to abandon Greek concepts tend to draw upon current philosophical systems whether existentialism or process philosophy to name but a few. Thus, each generation of theologians must re-evaluate its theological inheritance and engage with the philosophical systems of the day.

As we engage with contemporary philosophical systems and our social/cultural contexts, it is natural that we will reformulate our understanding of the faith that has been passed down to us from the ancient world. To give but one example, the way we envision God as the creator has been impacted by modern science, especially evolutionary theory. While we may find (and I do) the creation accounts theologically informative, they no longer provide a scientifically valid explanation of our origins. There are cultural adaptations that have taken place over the years, that have led to the rethinking of perspectives on the way we read Scripture and understand the nature of God. So, while we draw upon the witness of Scripture and Christian Tradition (history) when it comes to the nature of God, we must always keep in mind the distance that lies between us and the biblical and other ancient writers. The universe looks a lot different today than it did 2000 years ago. It's not that they were primitive thinkers, and we're advanced thinkers. Rather it is simply a matter of the accumulation of information that we have at our disposal as we consider how to speak of God.

In this brief study, I would like to introduce some of the basic concepts that Christians use to talk about God. My discussion should be seen as more descriptive than prescriptive. I hope that I can provide some definitions, language, and perhaps options, that might facilitate a more thoughtful discussion of how Christians might understand God's nature. While I could include in this book a discussion of the proofs of the existence of God, that might take us too far afield from what I have in mind. Therefore, while many would deny the existence of God, for our purposes I will start with the presupposition that God does exist. If that is the case, then what concepts and language are useful in expressing that belief?

We will begin in chapter one with the foundational premise/ confession that unites Christians, Jews, and Islam. This confession declares that there is but one God. In other words, these three faith traditions are by definition monotheistic. While Christians claim to be monotheists, most Christians (not all) also speak of God in trinitarian terms. Thus, the Christian version of monotheism is not as "pure" as our Jewish and Muslim cousins. We'll take up the topic of the Trinity in chapter two. This conversation will be followed by a discussion in chapter three of the attributes and character of God, noting, especially with the attributes of God, where there are significant differences in understanding. I have included a chapter on divine providence because it speaks to the nature of God's agency in the universe. In other words, how have Christians understood the ways in which God might achieve God's ultimate purposes for creation?

My goal in writing this book is to provide a brief but helpful guide to some of the key concepts and concerns that we encounter when we speak about God. While I will take note of Christological (Christian beliefs about Jesus) and Pneumatological (Christian beliefs regarding the Holy Spirit) elements of our God talk, especially when it comes to the Trinity, I will not be focusing specifically on Christology or Pneumatology.[1]

---

1 I explore in some depth the doctrine of the Holy Spirit and the Spirit's relationship to humanity in my book *Unfettered Spirit: Spiritual Gifts for the New Great Awakening,* 2nd ed., (Gonzalez, FL: Energion Publications, 2021).

CHAPTER 1

GOD IS ONE

The *Shema,* the Jewish statement of faith found in Deuteronomy 6:4 states: "Hear O Israel: The Lord is our God, the Lord
alone. You shall love the Lord your God with all your heart and
with all your soul, and with all your might." While Deuteronomy
speaks to the monotheistic foundations of the Jewish faith, the term
monotheism does not tell us much about God. Although the term
"monotheism" distinguishes Israel's faith from the polytheism of its
neighbors, it doesn't give us a full sense of Israel's understanding of
God. Brevard Childs notes that "equally important is to recognize
that the unity and uniqueness of God (Deuteronomy 6:4ff), which
calls for utter devotion—heart, soul, and might—did not denote
God's being as that of a monad, or of a monolithic, unchanging
deity. Rather, Israel developed a variety of hypostatic-like {*note: personal*} forms by which to bear witness both to God's transcendence
and his immanence."[2]

As we consider this monotheistic heritage, it is important
to note that it was an idea in development. Even passages in the
Hebrew bible that speak of God's oneness (Deuteronomy 6) may
not have emerged in a purely monotheistic context. Instead, while
early Jews may have assumed that for them there is only one God,
they may also have assumed that other deities existed. We see elements of this present in the Old Testament. The term used for such
a view is henotheism. As time passed, largely after the Babylonian
Exile (6th century BCE), Jews moved toward true monotheism.
Of course, as we'll see further on, Christians have modified monotheism in light of the doctrine of the Trinity.

When we affirm the oneness of God (monotheism) even in a
Trinitarian form (and not all Christians are Trinitarian), we affirm
our common Abrahamic heritage that is shared with Jews and Muslims. While Jews and Muslims have a purer form of monotheism
than is true of Christians (the Trinity complicates things for Chris-

---

2 Brevard Childs, *Biblical Theology of the Old and New Testaments: Theological
Reflection on the Christian Bible,* (Minneapolis: Fortress Press, 1992), p.
355

1

tians), all three faiths affirm that God is one. We may interpret this oneness of God differently, but this confession unites us.

GOD AS SPIRIT

The biblical witness speaks of God in terms of spirit. In the Gospel of John, Jesus speaks of those who worship God in "spirit and in truth" (John 4:24). If we think of God in terms of Spirit, we must be clear that almost all God language is analogical or metaphorical. Thus, it is important to remember that any gendered language used to describe God is not to be taken literally. God is beyond gender. Therefore, if we speak of God as Father, we speak analogically not univocally. That is, the term Father does not directly describe God's nature. That is because, as God reminds Hosea, "for I am God and no mortal" (Hosea 11:9). The issue of the relationship between God and gender requires our attention, because the use of masculine language for God has often been used to put women in a subordinate position to men. As we consider the biblical testimony about God, we need to remember that Israel rejected the fertility cults of its neighbors, cults that emphasized the gender of their gods and goddesses.

This issue of language goes for both male and female language. If one keeps in mind that our language for God cannot be taken literally, then we should be able to speak of God in male, female, or non-gender-related terms. Scripture also speaks of God using feminine imagery, which should be sufficient support for such uses today. Thus, God could be described as a mother crying out as if in the pain of labor (Isaiah 42:14); or as in Isaiah 66:13 God is described as having a maternal relationship with Israel: "As a mother comforts her child, so I will comfort you; you shall be comforted in Jerusalem." As Elizabeth Johnson points out, however, "Inherited Christian speech about God has developed within a framework that does not prize the unique and equal humanity of women, and bears the marks of partiality and dominance."[3] Thus,

---

3   Elizabeth Johnson, *She Who Is: The Mystery of God in Feminist Theological Discourse.* 10th Anniversary Edition, (New York, NY: Herder and Herder, 2002), p. 15.

we must keep ourselves aware of the nature of our God talk, which can easily become overly masculine.

GOD AS TRANSCENDENT AND/OR IMMANENT

When it comes to God's relationship with creation, we usually speak in terms of transcendence and immanence. We see expressions of both in Scripture, though the primary witness is that God, as Creator is separate from the rest of creation. God is the creator, and we are not. The question concerns how wide the divide between God and creation is. At one end of the theological spectrum, God is understood to be "wholly other" and thus exists completely outside the created order. In this perspective, God may choose to intervene supernaturally, which has been the primary vision of Christian theology and is present throughout the biblical materials. The most extreme version of this viewpoint that emerged in the age of the Enlightenment (17th/18th centuries) is deism, which presumes that once God created the universe, God left it to its own devices (though some philosophers believed that God might step in from time to time to tweak things—think a spinning top). At the other end of the spectrum, we have pantheism, a system of belief in which there is no separation between the divine and creation. If this is understood to be a continuum, then a significant option that has gained traction in recent decades is panentheism. That is, the world is in God, and God is in the world. While panentheism emphasizes God's immanence—God's close relationship with cre-ation—unlike pantheism, there is a differentiation between God and the created order.

In the biblical witness, God's transcendence tends to be emphasized. God is understood to be different from us not only in degree but in essence. We see this expressed in the opening verses of Genesis where God speaks creation into existence, declaring each expression good (Genesis 1:1ff). According to Augustine, who is a primary exemplar of classical theism, God created the universe out of nothing. Nothing can exist except God created it for God is omnipotent.[4] God is often pictured sitting on the throne of heaven,

---

4 Augustine, "Faith and the Creed," in *On Christian Belief*, (New York, NY: New City Press, 2005), p. 156.

high and lifted up, surrounded by angels (Isaiah 6:1-8). In classical theism God is understood to be self-sufficient, not requiring the world to exist for God to exist.

On the other hand, God is understood to be immanent, that is, present with and in creation. Consider the second creation story, where God creates the man from dirt and the woman from the man, and then later takes walks in the Garden (Genesis 2). In the New Testament, Paul told the Athenians that God "is not far from each one of us," and as proof, he quoted one of their own philosophers who said: "In him we live and move and have our being" (Acts 17:27-28). Jesus describes God as one who is actively involved in the created order, making the sun rise on both the evil and the good and bringing rain on both as well (Matthew 5:45).

If God is both distinct from us, but also close at hand, how might we understand the possibility of embracing both transcendence and immanence? How do we honor the declarations of God's holiness, while also embracing the relational nature of God? One solution to this apparent dilemma is found in the aforementioned "panentheism." Unlike pantheism, which merges God and the universe, panentheism suggests a middle ground—one that leaves room for God and the universe to both exist. With panentheism (note the "en" after pan) the world exists within but distinct from God. Another way of putting this is to suggest that the finite exists within the infinite. Regarding divine agency, God does not act from outside creation but within creation, for creation exists within God. Panentheism, like classical theism, comes in more than one form. However, it has become an important way for Christian theologians to envision God's relationship with the universe, especially in light of the revelations of modern science. What panentheism attempts to do is propose a way for God to be engaged in/with the universe without being identical to it and without the necessity of intervening from outside in a supernaturalist way—something that natural law would argue against, but which is assumed by classical theism.

GOD AS CREATOR

Genesis 1 is a hymn celebrating God the Creator, revealing at the very beginning of the story that God is the creator of all things,

4

and God did so by way of God's Word. And all that God creates is declared to be good. Psalm 19:1 confirms this message declaring: "The heavens are telling the glory of God; and the Firmament proclaims his handiwork." The message is that the created order is something different from God, though how God transcends what God creates is not revealed, only that God and creation are not the same. While humanity is created in the image and likeness of God, we are not God. As to whether God is understood to have created the universe out of nothing (*creatio ex nihilo*) or out of some pre-existing material is unclear, leading to differences of opinion that lie outside the bounds of this discussion.[5]

We'll get to the doctrine of the Trinity in a moment, but it's important to note that creation is usually understood to be a tri-une act. Thus, God is the initiator of creation, but it is through the Logos (Word) that God creates, and as the Gospel of John notes, this word by which God creates takes on human flesh and dwells among us (John 1:1-14). Christ's role in the act of creation is described with even greater clarity in Colossians 1:16-17: "For in him all things in heaven and on earth were created, things visible and invisible, whether thrones or dominions or rulers or powers— all things have been created through him and for him. He is before all things, and in him all things hold together."

We see the Holy Spirit present in the very beginning of the biblical story where we read that the Spirit's role in creation is that of "the divine power active in creating the universe." When it comes to the role of the Spirit in creation, we again turn to Genesis 1:2, which reveals that "the earth was formless and void and darkness covered the face of the deep, while a wind from God swept over the face of the waters" (Genesis 1:2 NRSV). While the NRSV translates the Hebrew word *Ruach* as wind, which is appropriate, the older Revised Standard Version offers a more traditional reading, such that "the Spirit of God was moving over the face of the

---

5 See David Moffett-Moore, *Creation in Contemporary Experience,* (Gonzalez, FL: Energion Publications, 2014), for a helpful discussion of a theology of evolution and other dimensions of this conversation. For a discussion of the scriptural dimensions of this conversation see Herold Weiss, *Creation in Scripture: A Survey of All the Evidence,* (Gonzalez, FL: Energion Publications, 2012.

waters" (Genesis 1:2 RSV). This is also an appropriate option. This passage speaks of God bringing order out of chaos. Perhaps we can see this as bringing order to the materials God already brought into being. Psalm 104:29-30 speaks of the dependence on the Spirit for life that we all have:

> Why you hide your face, they are dismayed;
> When you take away their breath they die,
> and return to their dust.
> When you send forth your Spirit they are created;
> and you renew the face of the ground.

While we need to be careful not to impose Trinitarian constructs on Scripture where they are not found, these passages, and others like them, at least suggest, even if they do not provide a definitive statement, that the Holy Spirit is part of the creative process.

Jürgen Moltmann provides us with this valuable statement on the Trinity in creation:

> The Christian doctrine of creation takes its impress from the revelation of Christ and the experience of the Spirit. The One who sends the Son and the Spirit is the Creator—the Father. The One who gathers the world under his liberating lordship, and redeems it, is the Word of creation—the Son. The One who gives life to the world and allows it to participate in God's eternal life is the creative Energy—the Spirit. The Father is the creating origin of creation, the Son its shaping origin, and the Spirit is the life-giving origin.[6]

Moltmann also points out that the Trinitarian foundation of the doctrine of creation brings together God's transcendence and God's immanence. If we overly focus on God's transcendence, we end in deism. If we over-emphasize immanence, we end in pantheism. The Trinitarian view brings these into balance. In this we recognize both that God creates the world, and therefore, stands apart from it, and that God has chosen to indwell his creation by his Spirit.

6 Jürgen Moltmann, *God in Creation: A New Theology of Creation and the Spirit of God,* Margaret Kohl, trans., (San Francisco: Harper and Row, 1985), 97-98.

Why did God create the heavens and earth? The answer varies, with some suggesting that creation is a necessary action on God's part. That is, God could not have done otherwise. Others insist that God did not need to create but choose to do so. Whether necessary or not, with the Creeds we confess that God is the maker of the heavens and the earth.

With that in mind, we can heed the call of the Psalmist to offer glory and honor to God the Creator. The Psalms continually point to the beauty and order of creation. This same idea is found also in Revelation 4:8-11. In this passage we see the heavenly beings standing before the throne of God praising God both day and night. In verse 11 the issue of creation comes to the fore. "You are worthy, our Lord and God, to receive glory and honor and power, for you created all things, and by your will they existed and were created" (Revelation 4:11). James McClendon makes this keen observation about the relationship of this heavenly worship and the experience of the church that received this word: "Here then, is a primitive Christian celebration of the creation. As its first readers would know all too well, Revelation sprang from the midst of a suffering church. While the heavenly elders sang creation's praise, earthly elders suffered exile, imprisonment, and martyrdom."[7]

Again, the biblical texts do not exactly tell us why God created the heavens and the earth, nor how God created the universe, but Scripture does tell us quite strongly that what God created is good. One need only look closely at Genesis 1 to see this is true. Even though sin and evil may exist in the world at present that in no way takes away from the fact that the created order is good and that it is part of God's will. Any theology that suggests that the created order is evil or less than good or that the only purpose for the earth is to provide a way station on the way to heaven stands contrary to the words of Scripture. God created the earth out of his love as a dwelling place for his creatures. The earth is simply that, it is a loving expression of God's creative being. While the created order is not necessary, it is a rightful expression of God's being.

---

7 James McClendon, *Systematic Theology: Doctrine,* (Nashville: Abingdon, 1994), 149.

Our confessions of faith and traditional portrayals of God tend to come in male idioms. While Scripture at times speaks of God in feminine terms, for the most part, it is masculine imagery. So, is God male? If so, does that mean men are superior to women? We would be wise to remember that our names for God are larger metaphorical. We use them to speak of what is invisible. Thus, it is quite appropriate to speak of God in nonpersonal terms such as Tillich's "Ground of Being." However, nonpersonal terms often leave us dry and wanting more. Thus, we turn to more personal terms. So, we typically end up with gender-related terms for God, even when we understand that God transcends gender. This is seen in the celebration of God the creator; God creates humanity in God's image as male and female (Genesis 1:26-27). Even if male imagery predominates, we are not limited to male metaphors/symbols. As Elizabeth Johnson— whose book *She Who Is* has proven helpful to my reflections—points out, we can stretch and expand our language and repertoire of images "by uttering female symbols into speech about divine mystery." If we do this, however, we must be careful not to take these symbols literally or using female stereotypes to speak of God. This usage, however, "challenges the idolatry of maleness in classic language about God, thereby making possible the rediscovery of divine mystery, and points to the recovery of the dignity of women created in the image of God."[8] Thus, we can consider references to Wisdom, which is identified with God and portrayed as a woman. The Greek word for wisdom is Sophia, which is feminine. But there are other more direct references such as God as mother. God speaks of crying out like a woman in labor (Isaiah 42:14). God comforts Israel as a mother comforts a child (Isaiah 63:13). In fact, Isaiah envisions God as a mother nursing her child, as an expression of divine compassion (Isaiah 49:15). God serves a midwife in Psalm 22. Ultimately, we must recognize that in Christian theology God's essence is incompressible, and thus transcends gender. However, we must be careful

---

8   Elizabeth A. Johnson, *She Who Is: The Mystery of God in Feminist Theological Discourse,* 10th Anniversary Edition, (New York, NY: The Crossroad Publishing Company, 2002), p, 45.

because our traditional God language tends to be masculine, and simply adding feminine traits to our description of God does not change the fact that God tends to be spoken of and understood in male terms. For that reason, Elizabeth Johnson suggests that to get to equivalency then "extended theological speaking about God in female images, or long draughts of this new wine, are a condition for the very possibility of equivalent imaging of God in religious speech."[9] This can be difficult because we're not accustomed to such imagery. Nevertheless, the constant use of masculine imagery reinforces patriarchy. Unless our God language is understood as a literal equivalency, it should be possible to move toward a broader vision of God and gender so that God is no longer understood in completely masculine terms.

---

9 Johnson, *She Who Is,* p. 57.

CHAPTER 2

THE TRIUNE NATURE OF GOD

The Christian understanding of God has been largely defined in Trinitarian terms. The Trinity is how most Christians have named God. We may be monotheistic, but Judaism and Islam have a much more consistent and narrow understanding of monotheism. It is a formulation of the church in its attempt to reflect faithfully on the biblical witness. But it was precisely by observing the unity and differentiation of God within the biblical revelation that the church was confronted with the Trinity. The divine subject, predicate, and object, are not only to be equated but also differentiated. Indeed, it is the doctrine of the Trinity which makes the doctrine of God actually Christian.[10]

Ultimately, as we will see, the need for a doctrine of the Trinity ultimately arose from the need to make sense of the church's affirmation of the divine sonship of Jesus Christ. The doctrine emerged from the need to "do justice to the Christ who was from the church's inception confessed as Lord." As Childs also notes that when nineteenth-century Christians lost interest in the doctrine of the Trinity their Christologies also began to blur and become distorted.[11]

TRINITY IN THE BIBLE

Christian theology is rooted in the Hebrew Bible, which declares that God is one. The question then for Christians has been whether one can find the roots of the Trinity in the Hebrew Bible. Christian theologians in the pre-modern era were very adept at finding those links. Using an allegorical method of interpretation often made this possible. Critical engagement with Scripture and with Jews requires us to be careful with how we read and appropriate these texts—for Judaism is not Trinitarian.

---

10 Brevard Childs, *Biblical Theology of the Old and New Testaments: Theological Reflection on the Christian Bible,* (Minneapolis: Fortress Press, 1992), 375.
11 Childs, *Biblical Theology,* p. 376.

Texts like Genesis 1:26 have proven especially intriguing for Christian reflection. The use of the plural in the phrase "let us make humankind in our image, according to our likeness" is at least suggestive of a plurality of some kind within God. Theologians have wondered what the word "our" means. Now, it is doubtful that the author(s) had Trinity in mind, but could the seeds be there? Is it appropriate for Christians to make use of this phrase in developing a Trinitarian theology?

While we must admit that there is no direct reference to the Trinity in the Hebrew Bible, there are passages that offer us a foundation for a fruitful conversation. This is especially true of passages that speak of "Wisdom," which is often personalized in the Psalms and Proverbs as "Divine Wisdom." Wisdom is usually conceived of in feminine terms. Wisdom is often depicted as being involved in the creation of all things (Proverbs 1:20-23; 9:1-6; Job 28; Ecclesiastes 24). There is the concept of "Word," or divine speech, which at times is personified (Psalm 119:89; Psalm 147:15-20; Isaiah 55:10-11). And then there is the "Spirit of God," who is depicted often as God's presence in the world, active in creation (Genesis 1:2); present in the life of the promised Messiah (Isaiah 42:1-3); and as an agent of the new creation (Ezekiel 36:26; 37:1-14). There is also the concept of *Shekinah* (another word that is feminine), which describes the means of God's dwelling in the world (Exodus 25:8; 43:9; Zechariah 2:10; 8:3). These passages don't make for a doctrine of the Trinity, but they leave open the possibility of a broader understanding of God's nature. What we need to remember is that whatever understanding we might have of these concepts and similar concepts, they must be understood in the context of the Old Testament insistence on the oneness or unity of God (Deuteronomy 6:4-5).

There are no explicit statements of a doctrine of the Trinity in the New Testament.[12] The doctrine is a theological construction that attempts to make sense of the biblical witness, especially those texts that affirm the primary relationship between Father and Son.

---

12 Though some would argue otherwise that the New Testament offers explicit references to the Trinity, as Chris Eyre argues, it is difficult case to make. See his book *A Holy Mystery: Taking apart the Trinity Topical Line Drives Volume 34*, (Gonzales, FL: Energion Publications), pp. 6-8.

The most explicit statement is the baptismal formula found in Matthew 28:19. In the Great Commission, Jesus commands his followers to make disciples, baptizing them in the name of the Father, Son, and Holy Spirit. While this is the only New Testament expression of this formula, it has become the standard formula for most churches. A second passage, 2 Corinthians 13:13 (14), is more helpful in defining the relationship, but it's not without its difficulties: "The grace of the Lord Jesus Christ, the love of God, and the communion of the Holy Spirit be with all of you." Romans 8:11 speaks to the relationship of Father, Son, and Spirit to the issue of the resurrection. "If the Spirit of him who raised Jesus from the dead dwells in you, he who raised Christ from the dead will give life to your mortal bodies also through his Spirit that dwells in you."

All Christians agree on the oneness of God. We hold this belief in common with our Jewish and Muslim kin, and yet the doctrine Trinity emerged from the Scriptural witness to a more complex understanding of that oneness. Affirmations of the full divinity of Christ and the person of the Holy Spirit required further development of that vision of God. While the fourth-century formulations might not be perfect, they have stood the test of time. Theologian Elizabeth Johnson captures the vision that the doctrine Trinity engenders in Christian theology:

At its most basic the symbol of the Trinity evokes a livingness in God, a dynamic coming and going with the world that points to an inner divine circling around in unimaginable relation. God's relatedness to the world in creating, redeeming, and renewing activity suggests to the Christian mind that God's own being is somehow similarly differentiated. Not an isolated, static, ruling monarch but a relational, dynamic, tripersonal mystery of love—who would not opt for the latter?[13]

---

13 Elizabeth A. Johnson, *She Who Is: The Mystery of God in Feminist Theological Discourse*, 10th Anniversary Edition, (New York, NY: The Crossroad Publishing Company, 2002), p. 192.

12

THE HISTORICAL DEVELOPMENT OF A TRINITARIAN VOCABULARY

One of the needs the church faced early in its existence, especially as the church spread in the Latin West, was a vocabulary that could express the emerging Christian understandings of God. Tertullian, a brilliant theologian, and apologist for the church, filled that void in many ways. We look to him for many of the terms that the church came to use to describe God. These terms include the very word trinity, which comes from the Latin *trinitas*. He also introduced the term substance (Latin—*substantia;* Greek *ousia*), to describe the essence of God. Speaking in Trinitarian terms, Father, Son, and Holy Spirit share one substance. The third term was *persona,* which he used to translate the Greek *hypostasis.* God is one in substance but still is encountered as three persons.

The next stage in the process came at the Council of Nicaea, which addressed conflicting understandings of the Trinity as espoused by two Alexandrian priests, Arius and Athanasius. While neither of these two men spoke at the council, it was their theological work that drove the conversation. In the end, the position espoused by Athanasius won the day. The question had to do with whether the son shared the same substance as the Father. While Arius denied that Jesus shared full divinity, insisting that this was the more biblical position, he lost the day, and the council embraced the term *homoousious* (of the same substance) to define the relationship of Father and Son. While the debate did not end at Nicaea, this position became normative for much of the church.

WAYS OF APPROACHING THE TRINITY

Although the foundational Trinitarian vocabulary was introduced in the third and fourth centuries, the conversation continues to this day. When it comes to Trinitarian theology, there are essentially two ways of approaching this question. The first view is called the Economic Trinity and the other is the Immanent Trinity. One focuses on God's external activity in bringing salvation to creation, and the other on God's internal identity. Both ways of approaching the question rely on the same formula that was espoused at Nicaea and later at Constantinople in the fourth century.

The reason why conversations about the Trinity often steer toward the "economic Trinity," is that it is more relatable. Talking about God's internal being is difficult to imagine. Talking about God meeting us as Trinity in Christ through the Spirit with the promise of salvation speaks to where we live our lives. When we talk of the economic Trinity, we're talking about God's role in the creation, redemption, and sanctification of the created order. These three activities, however, should not be seen as occurring sequentially. As Clark Williamson puts it: "in each moment of our lives God creates us anew, redeems us out of the narrowness and stupidity of the past, and calls us forward toward God's future with all God's friends."[14] It is through this doctrine of the Trinity that we name the God of Israel who meets us in Jesus Christ, especially as Jesus is known to us on the cross, and is present to us and empowering us, by the Holy Spirit.

When we think about the Trinitarian nature of God, one of the more intriguing images is that of the three visitors whom Abraham and Sarah encounter at the Oaks of Mamre (Genesis 18:1-15). Clark Williamson draws on this story that emphasizes hospitality to suggest that "the Trinity is a communion of equal persons (coequal, the tradition liked to say), and we are invited into such communion." He goes on to say:

We speak of God as one in order to make clear that God is not divided, not double-minded. We speak of God as three to affirm communion in God. Life is a blessing and well-being when all relations of domination and oppression are expelled. Communion among persons is the divine order and the intended human order of well-being. The fundamental intent of the doctrine of the Trinity is to protect an understanding of God as a profound relational communion. A relationship (not merely a relation) of authentic communion among God, human beings, and all God's creatures is the aim of God's work in the world.[15]

---

14 Clark Williamson, *Way of Blessing, Way of Life: A Christian Theology*, (St. Louis: Chalice Press, 1999), p. 118.
15 Williamson, *Way of Blessing*, pp. 126-127.

There is much more to be said about the Trinity. It is a concept that is full of possibilities. What I've shared so far is an expression of the "Economic Trinity." When we encounter God, we don't encounter God's inner being, we encounter God as God engages us, bringing shalom, which is healing, wholeness, and salvation.

So, how do we speak of God today? Many raise questions about the usefulness of Trinitarian language, especially in its traditional formulation. Naming God as Father, Son, and Holy Spirit can suggest that God is male and that males are superior to women. Even if we consider the Holy Spirit in feminine terms, this can easily lead to a top-down hierarchy that leaves not only the Son as second in line, but the Spirit as a third person, and sort of an afterthought. One of the recent formulas that has gained popularity is Creator, Redeemer, Sustainer/Sanctifier. The problem with this form is that contrary to the biblical witness it focuses totally on function; functions that each person of the Trinity is to express. Traditionally it has been held that "external works of God are indivisible." Clark Williamson, following William Placher, suggests as a solution the formula: "Father, Son, and Holy Spirit, Mother of us All."[16] Trinitarian language has also proven problematic for interfaith conversations. Both Jews and Muslims are much stricter in their monotheism. This language can be a stumbling block to these important conversations as well. Yet, as Miroslav Volf argues in his book *Allah*, we can have a fruitful conversation, for Christians as well as Jews and Muslims affirm the premise that God is one. We may differ in our understanding of that oneness, but not on the premise. At the same time, it requires humility on all sides to admit that our language for God is inadequate to God's full reality.[17]

As we consider the nature of God, a conversation that includes the name(s) we use, we must recognize that no name and no understanding can exhaust the possibilities. Thus, we must continue to push the boundaries. Whatever our theological formulas, they will not exhaust what we would confess as to who God might be.

---

16 Williamson, *Way of Blessing*, p. 115.
17 Miroslav Volf, *Allah: A Christian Response*, (San Francisco: Harper One, 2011), pp. 127-148.

CHAPTER 3

THE ATTRIBUTES AND CHARACTER OF GOD

Having reflected on the premise that God is one (chapter 1) and that for most Christians God is Triune (chapter 2), I would like to move on briefly to the question of God's attributes and God's character. I will treat both the attributes and the character of God in this chapter, but I will treat them separately. First, I will lift up several traditional attributes such as omnipotence and omnipresence, but I will lift up several others as well. Then under the category of character, I will speak of love, holiness, and divine relationality.

ATTRIBUTES OF GOD

Omnipotence

In the Old Testament, God appears to both Abraham and Jacob as *El Shaddai,* which is usually rendered as "God Almighty." In philosophical terms it has been common among Christians to say that God is omnipotent; that is, God all-powerful. God can do what God chooses to do. Whatever limits are placed on God are self-imposed, though we should assume that God's actions are limited by God's choices and character. The assumption is that God cannot contradict Godself or act contrary to God's character. Ultimately, when we speak of omnipotence we speak in terms of God's relationship with the world. That is, to say that God is omnipotent is to focus on God's ultimate power over the universe.

Medieval theologian William of Ockham provided a helpful distinction between two kinds of power possessed by God that help undergird the reliability and trustworthiness of God. For Ockham, for God to be omnipotent or almighty does not mean that God has the power to do everything, at least in the beginning of all things. While God could have done everything once, once God decides to do something that choice limits some other possible choices. Regarding these two kinds of power, the first form according to Ockham is *Potentia absoluta* (absolute power of God).

Ockham believed that all possibilities are open to God, but these possibilities face the limitation of the law of noncontradiction and God's nature. This is a fairly substantial limitation, especially if we embrace the assumption that God is love. The second form of power is *Potentia Ordinata* (ordained power of God). The second form rests on the first and it speaks of a more limited power that according to Richard Muller, "guarantees the stability and consistency of the orders of nature and of grace; distinct from the *potentia absoluta* according to which God can exercise the entirety of his power and effect all possibility."[18] Thus, once God chooses a direction, God can't do things differently. Thus, once God chose to create the universe, other choices were no longer available to God. To offer another example, God could have become incarnate as a woman from Ghana, but once God chose to become incarnate as a Jewish man, no other possible choices were available. Of course, one could argue here that the incarnation needn't be a one-time event. In general, however, most Christians have assumed that the incarnation in Jesus was a unique event.

Critics of the idea of divine omnipotence will point to questions about God's relationship to such things as the presence of evil, death, disease, and natural disasters in creation. They raise questions as to how God can be both loving and all-powerful, and yet seemingly unwilling to deal with such situations. The most prominent critical response to traditional understandings of God's omnipotence comes from proponents of the varying forms of Open and Relational Theology, including Process Theology. Process Theology suggests that God's power is limited to God's ability to persuade or influence. God can't do all things even if God had wanted. Whereas traditional orthodoxy might allow God to grant free will to humanity, Process theology assumes that free will is inherent to reality. Thomas Jay Oord suggests, similarly, that if love is, as he assumes, non-coercive, then God cannot be love and act coercively, as understood in traditional understandings of omnipotence. Oord

---

18 Richard Muller, *Dictionary of Latin and Greek Theological Terms*, (Grand Rapids: Baker, 1985), 231-232.

offers as an alternative the idea of amipotence, or the power of love, a power that is strong but not domineering or controlling.[19]

Perhaps it's best to follow the lead of theologian Joe Jones who suggests that it's best to use the biblical term almighty rather than omnipotence, which creates needless confusions. As he points out, helpfully, "if God is simply all the power there is, then there is no reality beyond or different from God" Additionally, to say that God has absolute power without limitation, then God's power is arbitrary and unrestricted. Thus, we would be best served by simply speaking of God as the Almighty. Thus, God has the power necessary to be God, superior to all other forms of power.[20] More needs to be said, but I will leave it there for now.

Omnipresence

To say that God is omnipresent means that God is present everywhere and at all moments in time. Though, as Daniel Migliore points out that this view of presence needs to be clarified. He writes that the "truth of God's omnipresence is that God is present everywhere but everywhere freely present. God is present when and where and how God pleases. God is present to all creatures and in all events, but not in the same way."[21] If we take Migliore's clarification to heart, then we can understand omnipresence to relate to God's presence in both time and place. For most Christians, that does not mean that God and reality are one and the same thing (pantheism), but that God is truly present wherever and whenever God chooses.

Eternality

Related to the idea of God's omnipresence is the question of God's eternality. That is, God is without beginning or end. This

---

19 Thomas Jay Oord, *Pluriform Love: An Open and Relational Theology of Well-Being*, (Nampa, ID: SacraSage Press, 2022), p. 169-172.

20 Joe R. Jones, *A Grammar of Christian Faith: Systemic Explorations in Christian Life and Doctrine*, Vol. 1, (Landham, MD: Rowman & Littlefield Publications, 2002), p. 219.

21 Daniel L. Migliore, *Faith Seeking Understanding: An Introduction to Christian Theology*, Third Edition, (Grand Rapids, MI: Wm. B. Eerdmans Publishing Company, 2014), (Kindle ed.), p. 90.

doesn't necessarily mean that God stands outside of time, but that God is faithfully present through time. Thus, there never has been nor ever will be a time when God does not exist. Therefore, there is no time before God. The experience of the people of faith means that we ought not to conceive of God's eternality as timeless and unchanging, but that with respect to time God is always present (omnipresence). As Daniel Migliore helpfully notes, "the true meaning of the eternity of the triune God is that God is everlasting. God's everlasting life is open to relationship with and participation in the temporal world. The good news of the gospel is that the eternal God has time for us."[22]

Omniscience

Omniscience speaks to the extent of God's knowledge. Nothing, Scripture suggests, is hidden from God's sight (Hebrews 4:13). The idea here is that God knows all things and that this knowledge is not bound by time. Thus, God knows the past, present, and future. When it comes to knowledge of the future there are differences in understanding within the Christian community. For some God, because God ultimately controls all things, everything, including our lives will go according to God's plan. Therefore, God knows all things. For others, God may not control all things, but God can foresee all things, and thus knows the future in its fullness. Those who embrace an open future would respond by saying that God knows all that there is to be known, but that would not include everything that will transpire in the future since the future remains open and thus unknown even to God.

Immutable

In saying God is immutable, one declares that God does not change. As with omnipotence, omniscience, and omnipresence, the doctrine of immutability has roots in Greek philosophy. Plato held that perfection is an unchanging reality. Therefore, if God is perfect then God cannot change. The Greeks believed that change implied incompleteness and that if one was to change one either had to get better or worse. Change presumes imperfection and

---

22 Migliore, *Faith Seeking Understanding*, (Kindle ed.) p. 90.

incompleteness. The concept of immutability also presumes that a perfect being cannot be affected by or changed by any outside force or person. That means when biblical passages speak of God's change of mind or suffering, these passages should be read metaphorically. For others, those passages that speak of God changing God's mind opens up the possibility that God is responsive to events, and thus God is responsive to our prayers. To say that God changes, for those who embrace an open and relational view of God, doesn't mean that God is unreliable, but that God is responsive. Tom Oord writes that from an open and relational perspective, it is helpful to distinguish between God's essence and God's experience, such that "God's essence is eternally unchanging; it's stable and steadfast. But God's experience changes moment by moment; it's flexible and forming. The divine experience is like the growing universe. It changes."[23] One finds a similar view in some forms of Eastern Orthodox theology, which distinguishes between God's essence, which is unknowable, and God's energies, which are knowable.[24]

Impassible

Related to immutability is the doctrine of impassibility. With impassibility not only does God not change, but God cannot suffer or have feelings. The Greek word we translate as impassibility is *apatheia*. As Joseph Hallman notes in his definition of impassibility: "A being that suffers is imperfect because it is under the control of another. Emotion seems to imply a lack of rational self-control. Hence, *apatheia* is attributed to the divine, and is thought of, especially by the Stoics, as an ethical idea."[25]

If God cannot suffer or change, what does this mean? For many theologians, this led to the idea that God is without passion or feelings. This leads, however, to questions about God's relation-

---

23 Thomas Jay Oord, *Open and Relational Theology: An Introduction to Life-Changing Ideas,* (Nampa, ID: SacraSage Press, 2021), pp. 38-39.
24 See Robert D. Cornwall, "Partnering with the Divine Energies," in *Partnering with God: Exploring Collaboration in Open and Relational Theology,* Tim Reddish, et al, eds., (Nampa, ID: SacraSage Press, 2021), pp. 59-62.
25 S.v. "Impassibility," by Joseph M Hallman, in *Encyclopedia of Early Christianity,* Everett Ferguson, ed., (New York: Garland, 1990).

ship with God's creation. For example, if God cannot be affected by anything outside Godself then how can we say that God is compassionate? Theologians suggested that while we might experience God's compassion, God does not feel compassionate toward us because God cannot be seen as vulnerable to feelings. Of course, this will influence the way we interpret passages that attribute feelings of love, anger, jealousy, or sorrow to God. Are these only metaphors? Such a view is not without its challengers; the most prominent being from within a spectrum of theologians under the Open and Relational umbrella. Those who take this position suggest that an impassible God is by nature unresponsive to creation. Such a God is unable to feel compassion or be influenced by others. Thus, in response, Thomas Jay Oord writes, Open and Relational theologians assume that "God suffers with those who suffer and rejoices with those who rejoice."[26]

CHARACTER OF GOD

We've looked at several attributes that have traditionally been applied to God. These expressions of what some call classical theism have roots in Greek philosophy, which influenced theological developments as the Christian faith moved outward from its Jewish origins. Another way of speaking of God's nature is to look at God's character. Here we will look at three expressions of God's character: love, holiness, and relationality.

Love

In 1 John 4:8, the author straightforwardly declares that God is love. One could understand this in at least two ways. First, one could speak of love as one quality that God possesses. Or we could say that God's essence is love. If we embrace the second definition, then God cannot not love. Whatever God does reflects who God is, and according to John, God is love. Therefore, God acts accordingly. This vision is reflected throughout Scripture. It is often described in terms of God's compassion and mercy. Thus, we read in the Psalms: "Gracious is the Lord, and righteous; our God is

---

26 Oord, *Open and Relational Theology*, pp. 50-52.

merciful" (Psalm 116:5). Or, as Jeremiah puts it: "Is Ephraim my dear son? Is he the child I delight in? As often as I speak against him, I still remember him. Therefore, I am deeply moved for him; I will surely have mercy on him says the Lord. "(Jeremiah 31:20). Of course, we can't forget that most famous of expressions of divine compassion—John 3:16: "For God so loved the world that he gave his only Son, so that everyone who believes in him may not perish but have eternal life." The text goes on to state that God did not choose to condemn the world but to save it through Jesus Christ.

Speaking of God in terms of love invites us to envision God in relational terms. Theologian Thomas Jay Oord speaks of the "uncontrolling love of God." According to his definition of love, it is noncoercive. Therefore, if God is love then God cannot coerce. That means God does not control. Instead, God collaborates with creatures. In this understanding of God, Oord writes that "love logically precedes power in God's nature. And the logical preeminence of love over sovereignty affects how we should think about God's ongoing creating and relating with creatures."[27]

Holiness

To claim that God is love often stands in contrast to the claim that God is holy. When we sing about God's holiness, we tend to envision God being high and lifted up (Isaiah 6:1-5). Holiness is often understood in terms of moral perfection and purity. Therefore, God is separate from an imperfect and impure creation. If there is to be reconciliation or restoration something must be done to atone for this impurity. As Paul writes in Romans, we all sin and fall short of God's glory. Fortunately, according to Paul, we are justified by God's grace through "the redemption that is in Christ Jesus." How this redemption takes place is the death of Jesus on the cross (Romans 3:23-25).

Another way of understanding God's holiness is found in Hannah's prayer (1 Samuel 2:1-10). Hannah says of God: "There is no Holy One like the Lord, no one besides you; there is no Rock like our God" (vs. 2). To say that God is holy does not mean that

---

27 Thomas Jay Oord, *The Uncontrolling Love of God: An Open and Relational Account of Providence,* (Downers Grove: IVP Academic, 2015), p. 148.

God is puritanical. Rather, it means that God is just. Consider Isaiah's description of God as the God of Justice (Isaiah 30:18). In this proclamation, Isaiah calls on God's people to continually seek justice for their neighbors. And as we read in the post-exilic portion of Isaiah: "Thus says the Lord: Maintain justice, and do what is right, for soon my salvation will come, and my deliverance be revealed" (Isa. 56:1).

Relationality

Most Christians think of God in relational terms. Why would we pray if we did not expect that we had a relationship with the one whom we address? We may not have personal conversations with God in the way that Moses or Elijah did, but we hope someone is listening. Consider these words from an old hymn:

He leadeth me: O blessed thought!
O words with heavenly comfort fraught!
Whatever I do, wherever I be,
still 'tis God's hand that leadeth me.
He leadeth me, he leadeth me, by his own hand he leadeth me;
his faithful follower I would be, for by his hand he leadeth me.

The hymn speaks of God leading us by the hand along the path of life. In other words, it celebrates the belief that we are not alone in our journeys. God is there by our side. The Psalms give voice to that sense of relationship, speaking of God in terms of being the good shepherd. When we walk with the Good Shepherd, we shall not want anything (Psalm 23).

Despite our devotional conceptions of God, traditional theology often leaves God looking static and impersonal. Even the confession that God is father might not be as helpful as we would assume, for many times fathers can be distant, non-engaged, or even not present. Traditional philosophical descriptions of God such as omniscience, omnipresence, omnipotence, impassibility, and immutability leave us with a God who is rather sterile and unapproachable. While this classic form of theism can leave us feeling less than inspired, Scripture tends to speak of God in dynamic and relational terms.

The two creation stories illustrate two visions of God. In one story God is transcendent, even wholly other. In Genesis 1 God speaks creation into existence. While God declares that all is good there is little hands-on effort. The second creation story, on the other hand, is much more relational. In Genesis 2 God's hands get dirty as God creates the first human from the dust of the ground. Once God has created the first humans, God engages in conversation with them. Using very anthropomorphic imagery, God walks in the garden with them. This anthropomorphic imagery, which we should take metaphorically, illustrates the relational component of God's interaction with creation. The God who creates is not Aristotle's "unmoved mover." Instead, God is an active agent in human affairs.

If God is relational, then that means we can become partners with God. This idea of collaboration is an important component of Open and Relational Theology. It is also a possible component of a concept found within Eastern Orthodoxy that distinguishes between God's essence, which is unknown and inaccessible, and God's uncreated energies, which can be known and experienced.[28] While Open and Relational Theology usually envisions God needing partners (remember that in Process Theology God influences but does not coerce), Orthodoxy assumes that God, in God's essence, is without the need of a partner. That God creates is an expression of God's will and love, but is not necessary, for God is complete in God's self. Nevertheless, whether this partnership with God is inherent or not, it does exist. It is expressed in the incarnation, as the Word that is God becomes flesh and dwells among us (John 1:1-14).

---

28 Cornwall, "Partnering with the Divine Energies," pp. 59-62.

CHAPTER 4

THE PROVIDENCE OF GOD

A keyword in our theological vocabulary is the term "providence." This term is rooted in concepts of divine sovereignty. It has implications for several doctrinal concepts, including creation, predestination, and eschatology. It is important to our discussion because it focuses on the question of purpose. Is there a purpose for human existence? Why are we here? What is our future? What does God have to do with these questions? How is God involved? With discussed some of these questions in previous chapters, but the concept of providence speaks to God's relationship to our lives. The term providence stems from a Latin term, *providentia,* and in its essence, the term means "to foresee" or "to provide." More specifically, in our context, providence speaks to the way God is seen to order the events of creation and its outflow. It speaks to questions of why things happen the way they do and where things seem to be going. It reflects the biblical message that God is faithful, and God will bring to completion what God promises. How and when that is to be determined, and could as we've seen involve our partnership in the process.

We see providence reflected in the words of the Psalmist who declares:

21 When my soul was embittered,
    when I was pricked in heart,
22 I was stupid and ignorant;
    I was like a brute beast toward you.
23 Nevertheless, I am continually with you;
    you hold my right hand.
24 You guide me with your counsel,
    and afterward you will receive me with honor.
25 Whom have I in heaven but you?
    And there is nothing on earth that I desire other than you.
26 My flesh and my heart may fail,
    but God is the strength of my heart and my portion forever. (Psalm 73:21-26 NRSVue).

THREE ASPECTS OF PROVIDENCE

Historically, providence played an essential role in theological discussions from the medieval period up through the 1800s. A key proponent of the doctrine was Thomas Aquinas, who said God's providential hand was the first cause. Since all actions needed a first cause, he understood God to be that first cause. The doctrine of providence also played an important role in 19th-century liberal theology. Although Newtonian physics undermined the medieval notion of God being the first cause, providence still seemed to be an important concept, even if its nature had to be seen in a different light. For instance, the Liberal embrace of the doctrine of progress, especially as it was lived out through Darwinian evolution, seemed to fit nicely with the doctrine. In the 20th century, the horrors of war, the holocaust, and the possibilities of mass destruction, have tempered enthusiasm for the doctrine. Many people question how one can hold to a doctrine of God's providential care when there is so much evil in the world. With these questions in mind, let us move on to the three aspects of providence: Preservation, Concurrence, and Governance.

1. PRESERVATION

This first point affirms God's role in creation but goes further to affirm God's role in sustaining and preserving creation. God is seen as the one who upholds creation. This is given voice in Colossians 1:17: "He himself is before all things, and in him all things hold together." Hebrews 1:3 also supports this concept: "He is the reflection of God's glory and the exact imprint of God's very being, and he sustains all things by his powerful word." The concept of preservation is also exemplified in the fact that God pours out the rain on the just and the unjust (Matthew 5:45). Thus, God brings the universe into existence, and by grace, God sustains this world.

In a post-Newtonian world, we no longer see preservation in terms of God keeping the world from lapsing into nothingness if God ceased to be active in creation. That is, we assume that natural laws sustain the world's existence without divine intervention. However, the concept of preservation is important today, not merely with regard to the physical or material universe, but also as an answer to the apparent meaninglessness of life. While atheism tells us that there is no meaning to history, and eastern religions on the whole look for meaning outside history, Christianity offers the hope that God has a purpose for the universe's existence. There is, therefore, an *eschatological* hope. We have confidence that there is a goal, and God will achieve that Goal.

2. CONCURRENCE

The doctrine of concurrence affirms that God cooperates with natural and secondary causes to bring about his desired end. That is God cooperates with us to enable us to act. This doctrine is perhaps the most controversial aspect of providence. We might see how this works by contrasting two expressions of Reformed theology, that is "Calvinist" and "Arminian" perspectives regarding providence. In a Calvinist view of providence, God cooperates with secondary causes, so that in essence God causes us to act as we do, though indirectly. We see this idea present in the doctrine of predestination. Arminians on the other hand, believe God is more permissive in the way God cooperates with creation. That is, they would allow creatures at least a degree of free will. Therefore, humans have more choices when it comes to how they live in this world. The difference between the two perspectives possibly could be understood by the illustration of God opening doors. A Calvinist would see God opening doors and in essence causing us to go through the door. An Arminian might see God opening doors but allowing us the freedom to choose whether we go through it.

Whereas medieval physics assumed that nothing acted without God's concurrence, modern physics no longer assumes this idea. However, the idea of concurrence remains important. Rather than seeing the doctrine in terms of physics, classical Protestant theologians understood concurrence in terms of the will. God concurs with and causes actions. Once again, however, today the question is one of who is ultimate. The idea of concurrence in essence allows for the concept of miracle. It affirms that God can choose to enter in and act in history directly.

While it appears that everyone acts autonomously, able to act however they wish, the Christian faith affirms that even in rebellion, we remain dependent on God. Therefore, evil does not have any ultimate status. Concurrence also serves as an affirmation of God's graciousness that is extended to the deserving and the undeserving.

Finally, this aspect of concurrence affirms that God has invited us to participate in bringing to completion God's program for the universe. Specifically, God calls for us to pray and engage in work in line with our prayers. As we obey God, God "concurs" with our actions, sanctifying them and employing them for the sake of the realm of God. In this, we enter into community with God and other believers who have likewise responded to God's invitation.

3. GOVERNANCE

The third aspect of providence is *governance*, which assumes that in keeping with God's grace and wisdom, God guides and governs all events and circumstances, such that God brings them to their proper goal. In other words, this understanding of governance affirms that God is sovereign in history. We see the idea of governance exemplified in a passage from Ephesians:

> [8b] With all wisdom and insight [9] he has made known to us the mystery of his will, according to his good pleasure that he set forth in Christ, [10] as a plan for the fullness of time, to gather up all things in him, things in heaven and things on earth. [11] In Christ we have also obtained an inheritance, having been destined according to the purpose of him who accomplishes all things according to his counsel and will, [12] so that we, who were the first to set our hope on Christ, might live for the praise of his glory. (Ephesians 1:8b-12 NRSVue).

The message here is that God has a plan, and a goal, and God will accomplish that goal in the fullness of time. It would seem that this passage teaches that the future is not completely open-ended. A useful word here is *teleological*, such that history is going somewhere. Now, that doesn't mean that God has full knowledge of the future, only that God has a goal and will work toward accomplishing that goal. We might use the analogy of a GPS here. While God may have an intended destination, there may be many adjustments along the way because of the choices we make along the way. The Process concept of a divine lure might fit such a view of divine providence. It's not controlling, but it is responsive while having a goal.

This third aspect of providence could also be seen present in the way the biblical story is presented. While God had an original purpose in mind when creating the universe, things didn't seem to go as planned (the Fall) and thus God began creating responses to that choice such that in the end God's ultimate purposes might be fulfilled. Thus, we see these responses revealed in terms of the call of Abraham, the covenant with Israel, the incarnation, the cross, the resurrection, and the church. Each offers a response such that creation might be moved toward the fulfillment of God's purposes. Thus, in the end, God will achieve victory even if God does not have complete control over the processes of history.

This truth is declared in 1 Peter 1:5, which speaks of our inheritance. This inheritance is being kept for us, "who are being protected by the power of God through faith for a salvation ready to be revealed in the last time." These words of hope offered to those whose faith is shaken promise that even in the face of evil, evil will not triumph. God can and does bring good out of evil. The greatest example of this is the cross itself. What was meant for evil, the death of God's son, God used to bring salvation to the world. While evil may seem to have the upper hand, it will not triumph. We may be perplexed as to why the evil ones prosper, but the doctrine of providence and God's governance, assures us that even though we may not see the complete triumph of God in this life, we can have hope that in the end, good will prevail (Psalm 73).

The concept of God's providence speaks to the issue of divine agency, as noted above, it raises another question, that of theodicy. I've noted the responses from Open and Relational Theology, which assumes that God does not have ultimate control over the universe. I've also noted that for others, hope for resolution lies in the future when God will bring all things to a close such that evil will be destroyed and the good will emerge victorious. There are others who embrace a dualism in which good is in a fight with evil, with the hope that God will ultimately prevail over the evil one (Satan). Answering these questions is difficult, and there is not space here to offer a suitable answer. However, I believe it is important and helpful to embrace a Triune response that presumes that God experiences the sufferings of creation. As Joe Jones writes: "The clear import of God's becoming human and suffering affliction from other humans and suffering finally an ignominious death on the cross. . .. No suffering of any creature, of whatever sort, happens without God's emphatic and suffering response."[29] I realize that this is not a sufficient response, but it is the best I can offer in this moment.

29 Jones, *A Grammar of Christian Faith*. P. 289.

CONCLUDING THOUGHTS

I wrote this little book to serve as a conversation starter. It should be clear by now that Christians affirm the existence of God and have a sense of who God is, at least in relationship to us. While some believe that the descriptions of God in Scripture should be taken literally, hopefully, I've dispelled that idea. Our language for God is ultimately metaphorical, for God's identity lies beyond our words and images. That doesn't mean our language is irrelevant. Especially when speaking of the Trinity it's important that keep our images and understandings of each person of the Trinity distinct, lest we fall into the trap of modalism. Key as well is the importance of keeping ever before us the relational nature of God. These relational images tend to be personal, reflecting human interactions and relationships. Thus, we speak of God as Father, Mother, and Friend. Ruth Duck suggests that in our use of these metaphors we use them together with other metaphors so that we "avoid the impression that God is a human being writ large and to recognize that God's love is greater than human love. Yet metaphors for God based on human relationships will surely always be useful in Christian worship."[30] This, of course, also raises the question of the use of gender-related images and metaphors for God. As we ponder these challenges of language and theologizing, I find attractive the distinction that many Orthodox Christians make between God's essence, which remains unknowable (transcendent) and God's energies or works, in which God is made known. It's easier in many ways to say what God is not than to say what or who God is.

What we can confess is that God is our creator, our savior, and our sustainer. We can speak of a relationship that God desires to have with creation. Elizabeth Johnson speaks of the "one relational God" as being "utterly transcendent, not limited by any finite category," but is also "capable of the most radical immanence, being intimately related to everything that exists. And the effect of divine

---

30 Ruth C. Duck and Patricia Wilson-Kastner, *Praising God: The Trinity in Christian Worship,* (Louisville, KY: Westminster John Knox Press, 1999), p. 31.

drawing near and passing by is always to empower creatures toward life and well-being in the teeth of the antagonistic structures of reality."[31] I find that description of God quite hope-producing. Ultimately, we move toward union with God who creates and loves us. Thus, as Vladimir Lossky writes "in the Parousia, and the eschatological fulfillment of history, the whole created universe will enter into perfect union with God. This union will be realized, or rather will be made manifest, differently in each of the human persons who have acquired the grace of the Holy Spirit in the Church. But the limits of the Church beyond death and the possibilities of salvation for those who have not known the light in this life, remain a mystery of the divine mercy for us, on which we dare not count, but to which we cannot place any human bounds."[32] This is, of course, the mystery of faith.

---

31 Elizabeth A. Johnson, *She Who Is: The Mystery of God in Feminist Theological Discourse,* 10th Anniversary Edition, (New York, NY: The Crossroad Publishing Company, 2002), p. 229.
32 Vladimir Lossky, *The Mystical Theology of the Eastern Church,* (Crestwood, NY: St. Vladimir's Seminary Press, 1957), p. 235.

Topical Line Drives

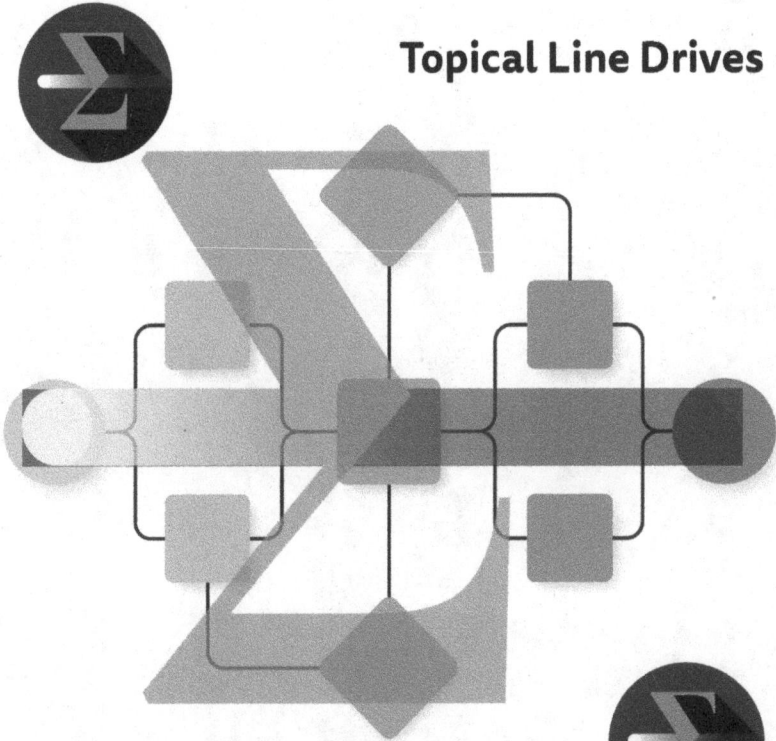

Straight to the point in 44 pages
https://topicallinedrives.com

www.ingramcontent.com/pod-product-compliance
Lightning Source LLC
Chambersburg PA
CBHW011749020426
42331CB00014B/3339

* 9 7 8 1 6 3 1 9 9 8 5 4 6 *